HORIZONS

edited by John Fairfax

EDWARD ARNOLD

First published 1971
by Edward Arnold (Publishers) Ltd,
41 Maddox Street,
London, WIR OAN

ISBN: 0 7131 1650 1

Printed in Great Britain by
Western Printing Services Ltd, Bristol

Contents

Introduction

These are a few of the printable remarks I've heard when people learn I write verse.

At an American Air Base where I was giving a reading from my poems some of the flyers came up to me during an interval and said, 'We expected an old man with long white hair and a cape. Heck, you even drive a sports car.'

Misconceptions about poets follow as wide a pattern as misunderstandings about poetry.

Not all poets are dead. Nor are they necessarily old men. This selection of contemporary poetry is compiled from the work of poets of widely differing age groups.

Some lyrics of the best popular songs might be called poetry. And some poets I know write poems that are sung. Which is not saying the same thing.

That poetry is once again being heard (readings by poets are on the increase) is a good sign, for it means among other things that the ear as well as the eye is brought to work. Listening to a poem often brings a further dimension to one's understanding of it. And you don't need a pretty accent to read a good poem.

Poets pass nowadays, open-eyed and listening, through as many departments of life as there are departments in life. And when they put pen to paper they do so with love and knowledge of language and imagination.

Poets are birds of the air, fish of the sea, animals in the landscape and the men, women and children in the days and years of language.

This book is a selection of contemporary poetry put together to demonstrate how the creative imagination of poets of the second half of the twentieth century is keeping a language alive and flourishing. Our language. The language we and they are responsible for handing on to future generations so that they in their turn may wrestle with communication and understanding.

It is our heritage and responsibility to hand on our language as bright and sharp as we can possibly make it.

It must be strong and full of energy if it is to express the multifarious thoughts and emotions, complex or simple, that future generations will need to tackle. It is the language they will use to make love, to cajole, to humour, to teach, to placate, to explain, to understand; and in their turn they must pass on brighter and stronger than we left it.

You and I may splutter and stammer over a counter while buying bootlaces but nevertheless we are using language.

Fundamentally the poets in this book are using the same language as anyone else. But what they do with it is a different matter.

Poetry is the jewel of language and language is one of the corner-stones on which civilisation is built.

The poems in this book are, like any work of art, works of imagination. They are from twentieth-century British poets who are using our language not like men worried by what they say, nor as a piece of diplomatic equipment to gloss over unpleasant truths, but in such a way that language and the rhythm of language can express responsibly, honestly and exactly, the traumas and vicissitudes of our lives and thoughts, our emotions and our feelings.

To illustrate something of the workings of a poem I will complete this introduction with the note-book draft of one of my own poems and the broadcast version of the completed poem.

Lundy Poem 4 is one of a sequence of poems I wrote on or soon after visiting Lundy Island.

This is a 'found' poem. That is to say I stumbled on it, almost literally, as I was walking one day with a friend along a track following the western edge of the cliffs. We came upon a large rock some eight to ten feet high, and on the top of this rock I could see a smaller boulder perched. This aroused my curiosity—especially as the large rock was throned at the top of steep cliffs with an uninterrupted view into the western horizon.

I do not know what urged me to clamber on to the large rock—I think I had the childish idea of rolling the small boulder down the cliff into the white waves smashing against its base. When I had climbed the rock, however, I found the small boulder to be special. A surface had been sliced flat and polished with a carefully carved epitaph cut simply into the granite.

> Wendy Anne Mitchell,
> Poet, aged 21,
> Who died on Lundy, 9th July, 1952.

On the cliff's edge
I stand ~~looking over~~ overlooking Halftide Rock
Upon the ~~cursed~~ sea proud g[?] Atlantis
In my ears the ~~mournful~~ moaning[?] psalm
Peels from the Rock islands
Echoed by basking seal
And I feel the hand of
the virgin poet touch mine
As she falls again ≠ again
Onto the cruel rock

that are ~~like~~ the Southern
~~suggestin~~ portal
Of Atlantis where she is poet
~~Priestless~~ of the seas.
~~How of these sea islands.~~
Of the paradise only the
Young & proud may know

Wendy Anne Mitchell.

Sheltering behind the large rock from Atlantic winds I put the first words of this poem into my note-book.

Later and over the next few days, then during the following weeks—miles away on the mainland—I worked the verse into shape, and four months later the B.B.C. broadcast the poem as it appears at the end of this introduction.

I have said that this poem was 'found' because it is likely that had I not been curious and climbed the large rock I might never have happened on the epitaph of the girl poet who fell to her death from Lundy Island.

Many poets 'find' poems—as poems visit poets. A poet may see something that triggers his imagination as he walks along a crowded street. Or a dustering of birds over a summer wood may move words from his imagination to the page.

Reading the note-book draft you will perhaps see that the words were written hard and urgently, pinning the first ideas as they came to me. From these lines written in the shelter of a rock I was able at a later time to reimagine the circumstances accurately and to embody the verse with more clarity and more strength by tightening the language and setting the shape of the words into a more fluent and distinct structure.

But whether or not *Lundy Poem 4* works in the long run is something only readers will decide. If it touches one reader's imagination and lets him see for a moment Wendy Anne Mitchell's death on Lundy Island then maybe . . .

> 'Wendy Anne Mitchell,
> Poet, aged 21,
> Who died on Lundy, 9th July, 1952.'
>
> I stand on the cliff's edge
> Overlooking Halftide Rock
> Down a searoad to the Atlantic.
>
> In my ears a moaning psalm
> Peels from Rock Island
> Echoed by basking seal,
>
> And I feel the hand
> Of the virgin poet touch mine
> As she falls again and again
>
> Onto the calling rocks
> That are the Eastern portal
> Of the ocean where she is poet
>
> Of 'the paradise that only we
> The young and proud may know.'

John Fairfax

Hermitage, Berkshire

Acknowledgements

Acknowledgements for permission to reprint copyright poems are due to the following authors and publishers:

A. M. Heath & Co. Ltd for Michael Baldwin's 'Recognition' from *How Charles Egget Lost His Way* and 'My Position'; Macmillan & Co. Ltd for Patricia Beer's 'Lemmings' from *Just Like the Resurrection* and Alan Brownjohn's 'Farmer's Point of View' from *The Lions' Mouths*; Scorpion Press for D. M. Black's 'Left Hand' and 'With Decorum' from *With Decorum*; Barrie & Jenkins Ltd for D. M. Black's 'Document of an Inter-Stellar Journey' from *The Educators* and John Moat's 'Three Trees' and 'Song' from *Thunder of Grass*; Chatto & Windus Ltd for Alan Bold's 'A Memory of Death' from *A Perpetual Motion Machine*, Patric Dickinson's 'The Taxi-Driver' from *This Cold Universe* and Jon Stallworthy's 'The Almond Tree' from *Root and Branch*; Edinburgh University Press for G. M. Brown's 'Horse' and 'The Finished House', Tom McGrath's 'Night Songs' and Edwin Morgan's 'In the Snack Bar' from *Scottish Poetry Number One*; David Higham Associates Ltd for Charles Causley's 'The Question' from *Underneath the Water* and 'Nursery Rhymes of Innocence and Experience'; Methuen & Co. Ltd for Jack Clemo's 'Gulls Nesting Inland' from *Cactus on Carmel*; Longman Group Ltd for Brian Higgins' 'Neither Nor' from *Notes While Travelling*; André Deutsch Ltd for Geoffrey Hill's 'Annunciations' from *King Log*; Methuen & Co. Ltd for D. Holbrook's 'Mending the Fire' from *Object Relations*; Faber & Faber Ltd for Ted Hughes' 'Second Glance at a Jaguar' from *Wodwo*; Peter Levi, sj for 'Pancakes for the Queen of Sheba'; Jonathan Cape Ltd for Christopher Logue's 'Cats are Full of Death' from *New Numbers*; Edward Lucie-Smith for 'May-Fly'; Jonathan Cape Ltd for Roger McGough's 'The Fight of the Year', 'Poem about the Sun Slinking Off and Pinning up a Notice' from *Watchwords*; Cape Goliard Press Ltd for Michael Mackmin's 'Alter and Invent'; John Moat for 'Four Quarters'; Calder & Boyars Ltd for Robert Nye's 'Fishing' and 'Bat in a Box' from *Darker Ends*; George Allen & Unwin for Brian Patten's 'The Prophet's Good Idea' and 'Diary Poem' from *Notes to the Hurrying Man*; Sidgwick & Jackson Ltd for Jeremy Robson's 'While Reading on the Underground' from *Thirty-three Poems*; Gerald Duckworth & Co. Ltd for Paul Roche's 'Mother Goose Gone Grim' from *To Tell the Truth*; Vernon Scannell for 'Incendiary' from *A Sense of Danger*; Chatto & Windus Ltd for Jon Silkin's 'The Child' from *Poems New and Selected*; Oxford University Press for Jon Stallworthy's 'Letters to My Sisters' from *Out of Bounds* and Anthony Thwaite's 'Ali Ben Shufti' and 'Personal Effects' from *The Stones of Emptiness*; Penguin Books Ltd for Nathaniel Tarn's 'The Life We Do not Lead' from *Penguin Modern Poets 7*; Jonathan Cape Ltd for D. M. Thomas' 'The Lost Forest' from *Two Voices*; and The Bodley Head for Rosemary Tonks' 'Farewell to Kurdistan' and 'Song of the October Wind' from *Iliad of Broken Sentences*.

Brian Patten

The Prophet's Good Idea

A new prophet appeared recently; was first seen
walking out an ocean. Which? We've forgotten.

He said
to the hushed crowds that had gathered, to
the journalists, the radio and television newscasters,
the Look at Life team and the politicians:
'Stay in Bed.'
That was his message. 'Bring each other
cups of coffee;
lie naked as near as possible without touching,
think of governments, chewing-gum, wars,
Queen Elizabeth coronation cups, anything—
you're bound finally to burst out laughing.
Draw peace maps across each other's bodies.
Climb into bed. Imagine if everyone did.
Returning astronauts would hear
only the sound of dreaming.'

Well the hushed crowds, the journalists, the
radio and television newscasters,
the Look at Life team and the politicians
thought it sounded a good message; a clear message,
the kind they could pass on
quite harmlessly to children.
Bed manufacturers were informed.
They loved the idea, loved it. Made beds big enough
to hold several hundred people
thinking of chewing-gum, Queen Elizabeth coronation cups,
anything—

'It sounds so good a message,' said the people,
'that something's bound to be wrong. . . .'
So philosophers, house-hold names and a TV personality
gathered to discuss the message. There were
a few flaws to be ironed out—
Robots were to be invented for the menial task
of running the planet—otherwise, a fine message.

And so now the whole planet's sleeping;
East and West snores, Hansel and Gretel personified.
Moss and moonwort burst out from bank-vaults;
all manner of creatures make themselves at home in houses;
from bed to bed spiders spin their webs, dream-catchers.

1

And there are sleep-walkers and sleep-lovers
in nightgowns or pyjamas, in underwear or nothing,
wandering through fields or suburbs, all so quietly.
And some woken from nightmares sit and comfort one another
whispering, *and o, it's all madness!*

                              And occasionally
the prophet rising from his ocean
drifts down the inland currents, watches whatever moves.
Occasionally drags himself up into radio-ships
where earphones to his brain he listens,
makes sure it is all still silent.
And o it's all madness and he has little else to do
him suffering from insomnia,
adrift in his faery-tale silence.

Patric Dickinson

This Cold Universe

These stars and planets have no names,
To name them is to lie,
I stare at this cold universe
So far from me so near to me.

How should I tame the Bear?
How steer the Plough?
I stare at this cold universe
I see into your eyes.

Above the Fell they throb and wheel
As my heart in its darkness does,
I stare at a colder universe
When I look into myself,

Marking distance, mapping void
With small 'good things of day.'
I stare at the cold universe
I reach out for your hand.

What measure is there else?
Light-years in a touch.
I stare into the darkness of myself
Where all lights may be false

Daydreams seen from a dry well—
One must have none of these
But measure the cold universe
By your mortal kiss.

Nothing must be but the sheer truth
Of love between us two:
O hand and planet eye and star
So near to me so far from me.

Nursery Rhyme of Innocence and Experience

I had a silver penny
  And an apricot tree
And I said to the sailor
  On the white quay

'Sailor O sailor
  Will you bring me
If I give you my penny
  And my apricot tree

'A fez from Algeria
  An Arab drum to beat
A little gilt sword
  And a parakeet?'

And he smiled and he kissed me
  As strong as death
And I saw his red tongue
  And I felt his sweet breath

*'You may keep your penny
  And your apricot tree
And I'll bring your presents
  Back from sea.'*

O the ship dipped down
  On the rim of the sky
And I waited while three
  Long summers went by

Then one steel morning
  On the white quay
I saw a grey ship
  Come in from sea

Slowly she came
  Across the bay
For her flashing rigging
  Was shot away

All round her wake
  The seabirds cried
And flew in and out
  Of the hole in her side

Slowly she came
  In the path of the sun
And I heard the sound
  Of a distant gun

And a stranger came running
  Up to me
From the deck of the ship
  And he said, said he

'*O are you the boy*
  Who would wait on the quay
With the silver penny
  And the apricot tree?

'*I've a plum-coloured fez*
  And a drum for thee
And a sword and a parakeet
  From over the sea.'

'O where is the sailor
  With the bold red hair?
And what is that volley
  On the bright air?

'O where are the other
  Girls and boys?
And why have you brought me
  Children's toys?'

Jeremy Robson

While Reading on the Underground

for Dannie Abse

I start at the rude intrusion
of a voice (as when the morning
light intrudes upon a dream):
'Stand clear of the doors.'
Piccadilly slaps me in the face.

Two stops to go. Once more I sink
into the poem: fields stir again,
birds commence their frantic psalms.
Their power grips my body—
no use. Covent Garden calls.

The office world takes over.
Feet (reminder of six million pairs
of stamping feet) stampede along
the corridors, commandeer the lift,
step out into the impartial streets.

Slowly now, slowly, through the market,
past lines of dispirited peaches,
not-quite-rosy apples, and marble pears
(pale imitations of the fruits you spoke about)

up the stairs, into the office, where
dull Monday faces already sear blank walls.
No 'Good morning' for the morning
is not good. No inspiration here.

Birds, fields, they seem a fable now—
though your urgent voice still
echoes, and re-echoes, in my mind.

Edwin Morgan

In the Snack-bar

A cup capsizes along the formica,
slithering with a dull clatter.
A few heads turn in the crowded evening snack-bar.
An old man is trying to get to his feet
from the low round stool fixed to the floor.
Slowly he levers himself up, his hands have no power.
He is up as far as he can get. The dismal hump
looming over him forces his head down.
He stands in his stained beltless gaberdine
like a monstrous animal caught in a tent
in some story. He sways slightly,
the face not seen, bent down
in shadow under his cap.
Even on his feet he is staring at the floor
or would be, if he could see.
I notice now his stick, once painted white
but scuffed and muddy, hanging from his right arm.
Long blind, hunchback born, half paralysed
he stands
fumbling with the stick
and speaks:
'I want—to go to the—toilet.'

It is down two flights of stairs, but we go.
I take his arm. 'Give me—your arm—it's better,'
    he says.
Inch by inch we drift towards the stairs.
A few yards of floor are like a landscape
to be negotiated, in the slow setting out
time has almost stopped. I concentrate
my life to his: crunch of spilt sugar,
slidy puddle from the night's umbrellas,
table edges, people's feet,
hiss of the coffee-machine, voices and laughter,
smell of a cigar, hamburgers, wet coats steaming,
and the slow dangerous inches to the stairs.
I put his right hand on the rail
and take his stick. He clings to me. The stick
is in his left hand, probing the treads.
I guide his arm and tell him the steps.
And slowly we go down. And slowly we go down.
White tiles and mirrors at last. He shambles
uncouth into the clinical gleam.

I set him in position, stand behind him
and wait with his stick.
His brooding reflection darkens the mirror
but the trickle of his water is thin and slow,
an old man's apology for living.
Painful ages to close his trousers and coat—

I do up the last buttons for him.
He asks doubtfully, 'Can I—wash my hands?'
I fill the basin, clasp his soft fingers round the soap.
He washes, feebly, patiently. There is no towel.
I press the pedal of the drier, draw his hands
gently into the roar of the hot air.
But he cannot rub them together,
drags out a handkerchief to finish.

He is glad to leave the contraption, and face the stairs.
He climbs, and steadily enough.
He climbs, we climb. He climbs
with many pauses but with that one
persisting patience of the undefeated
which is the nature of man when all is said.
And slowly we go up. And slowly we go up.
The faltering, unfaltering steps
take him at last to the door
across that endless, yet not endless waste of floor.
I watch him helped on a bus. It shudders off in the rain.
The conductor bends to hear where he wants to go.

Wherever he could go it would be dark
and yet he must trust men.
Without embarrassment or shame
he must announce his most pitiful needs
in a public place. No one sees his face.
Does he know how frightening he is in his strangeness
under his mountainous coat, his hands like wet leaves
stuck to the half-white stick?
His life depends on many who would evade him.
But he cannot reckon up the chances,
having one thing to do,
to haul his blind hump through these rains of August.
Dear Christ, to be born for this!

Nathaniel Tarn

The Life we do not Lead

The life we do not lead
looks down on us from both these banks and laughs
as Westminster delivers us into this tossing boat;

the life we do not lead
has the sleek hulls of ships moored to each bank
strange in our need as women and just as ignorant

of what they will put down;
the life we do not lead
keeps the sharp beaks of gulls to tear with and these wings

to beat itself to puffs of smoke in time for Charing Cross;
the life we do not lead
cannot be numbered as the Tower's stones

yet we evoke it corking down the Thames
freezing in this late Spring, pretending Summer
smells somewhere like these boats—

What do I make of this, you know, our being bound,
bound by the life we really lead and down at heel
(our boots cold fudge where slippers tripped the Globe)

in Shakespeare's year, and pitch so thin in England?
From here ships sailed that bound the mummy world,
great spiders on the wind, their sails like spider webs

and held the huge Pacific in those sails
as I hoard all the dreams the spinner heart can weave—
the life we do not lead

shrinks to a matchbox tossed on a minor sewer
as we, led by the lives that part us, abdicate,
melting into a mush for fish who've never even seen the sea.

Rosemary Tonks

Song of the October Wind

A mighty air-sea, fierce and very clean,
Was gliding in across the city.
Oxygenating gusts swept down and
Chloroformed us, in a light too bright to see by.

On pavements—china and milk pages
In a good book, freshly iced by the printing press—
October flash-floated. And you and I were moving
With alert, sane, and possessive steps. At home,

My sofa wrote her creaking, narcoleptic's Iliad.
My bathroom drank the Styx (bathwater
Of the Underworld). My telephone took all its voices
And gave them to the Furies, to practise with.

While slowly—to gigantic, muddy blows of music
From a pestle and mortar—roof, floor, walls, doors,
My London, stuffed with whisky-dark hotels,
Began to pant like a great ode!

And threw, carelessly, into our veins
Information—all the things we needed to know.
For which there are no words, *not even thoughts*.
And this was an ode shaken from a box of rats.

The first sky from October's aviary
Of bone-dry, thudding skies, joyful, free, and young,
With its wings lifted our souls, heavy as cities,
Effortlessly. We were trustworthy again.

Ritz, Savoy, Claridge's, hotels full of peacock words.
Were beaten white by Boreas; and as
Electric frosts scratched the windows
Fitting in their awkward childish pane of glowing stone.

We—copied the foaming *with our souls*!
The same ode tore the streets inside us. And lit
Catwalks, sofas, taxis in that city with a light
So bright, even the blind could see by it.

David Holbrook

Mending the Fire

A soft cold spring rain: where the gutter drips
I pause, waiting my time between the drops.
Over the shed roof with its grey stone-crops
A pale face at the pane, a gesture at its lips,

I wave, then you are gone, and I am in the dark,
And pause among the coal. A withered stalk
Breaks as I shovel at the wall: a paper keck
That white and viable once rooted in a crack

And grew indoors, and died, last summer, in the heat.
'Is there no more in life than this?' I think as I put out the light,
Bearing our crumb of comfort for the cool March night.
'If I am more than this dried thistle, what then, what?'

You are no longer at the window: a sudden gust
Plucks at me as I catch the latch in haste:
Then, as I walk along the house, carrying coals in, just,
I hear your voice, and the sad vacant mood is past.

But in that moment between outhouse and door
I saw our lintel break, the house drift out from shore
And sail away into a waste of time—as on the fire
We pile old forests now, or as the thistle failed to flower.

Nothing was left, as the rain rinsed my cheeks
Like unquenched tears, as by a grave grief breaks.
The new fire mends, and solemnly each makes
A love to each by glances, deeper than love that speaks.

Vernon Scannell

Incendiary

That one small boy with a face like pallid cheese
And burnt-out little eyes could make a blaze
As brazen, fierce and huge, as red and gold
And zany yellow as the one that spoiled
Three thousand guineas worth of property
And crops at Godwin's Farm on Saturday
Is frightening—as fact and metaphor:
An ordinary match intended for
The lighting of a pipe or kitchen fire
Misused may set a whole menagerie
Of flame-fanged tigers roaring hungrily.
And frightening, too, that one small boy should set
The sky on fire and choke the stars to heat
Such skinny limbs and such a little heart
Which would have been content with one warm kiss
Had there been anyone to offer this.

D. M. Black

Left Hand

Is an unweeded garden.

Is a baulk
        of anonymous timber.
Encrustation of slime and barnacles.

With a bone-handled knife
I shall whittle it
        to a boat of white wood,
a light boat at rest among shavings,
in a perfunctory clearing, among straggled, overblown roses.

Rosemary Tonks

Farewell to Kurdistan

As my new life begins, I start smiling at the people around me,
You would think I'd just been given a substantial meal,
I see all their good points.
The railway sheds are full of greenish-yellow electricity,
It's the great mid-day hour in London . . . that suddenly goes brown.
. . . My stupefying efforts to make money
And to have a life!
Well, I'm leaving; nothing can hold me.

The platforms are dense to the foot,
Rich, strong-willed travellers pace about in the dark daylight,
And how they stink of green fatty soaps, the rich.
More dirty weather . . . you can hardly see the newspaper stand
With its abominable, ludicrous papers . . . which are so touching
I ought to laugh and cry, instead of gritting my teeth.

Let me inhale the filthy air for the last time,
Good heavens, how vile it is. . . . I could take you step by step
Back among the twilight buildings, into my old life . . .

The trains come in, boiling, caked!
The station half tames them, there's the sound of blows; the uproar!
And I—I behave as though I've been starved of noise,
My intestine eats up this big music
And my new bourgeois soul promptly bursts into flames, in mid-air.

No use pouring me a few last minutes of the old life
From your tank of shadow, filled with lost and rotten people,
I admit: the same flow of gutter-sugar to the brain . . .
I admit it, London.

No one to see me off—Ah!
I would like to be seen off; it must be the same agonizing woman
Who does not want to understand me, and who exposes me in
public,
So that I can turn away, choked with cold bile,
And feel myself loved absolutely; the bitch.

These carriages, that have the heavy brown and black bread
Up their sides! But look out for the moment of cowardice,
It's Charon's rowing-boat that lurches and fouls my hand
As I climb on—exile, Limboist.

. . . The way these people get on with their lives; I bow down
With my few deeds and my lotus-scars.
Last minutes . . . last greenish-yellow minutes
Of the lost and rotten hours . . . faro, and old winters dimmed,
On which the dark—Yes, the black sugar-crust is forming, London.

I'm leaving! Nothing can hold me!
The trains, watered and greased, scream to be off.
Hullo—I'm already sticking out my elbows for a piece of territory,
I occupy my place as though I can't get enough of it
—And with that casual, haughty, and specific gestures, incidentally.

Tradesmen, Pigs, regenerative trains—I shall be saved!
I shall go to the centre of Europe; gliding,
As children skate on the diamond lid of the lake
Never touching ground—Xenophile, on the blue-plated meadows.

Oh I shall live off myself, rainclothes, documents,
The great train simmers. . . . Life is large, large!
. . . I shall live off your loaf of shadows, London;
I admit it, at the last.

Patric Dickinson

The Taxi-Driver

He said, '*When I retire*
'*I want to get out further*,
'*I want to get to the earth.*'
And I thought, not even death
Guarantees you earth; we have changed
Death's element to fire.

And your children, do they know
There's earth still under cities?
The bombs dug it up, seeds
Blew in for miles, weeds rooted.
Then men put in their perennial,
Money: now watch it grow.

You want to get to the earth
Only twenty miles from here;
Some want to get out further,
To the Moon, to Mars, to escape
It may be from earth-murder.
Which is harder? Which more worth?

Roger McGough

Soil

we've ignored eachother for a long time
and I'm strictly an indoor man
anytime to call would be the wrong time
I'll avoid you as long as I can

When I was a boy
We were good friends
I made pies out of you
When you were wet
And in childhood's glorious
Summer weather
We just roughandtumbled together
We were very close

just me and you and the sun
the world a place for having fun
always so much to be done

But gradually
I grew away from you
Of course you were still there
During my earliest sexcapades
When I roughandfumbled
Not very well after bedtime
But during my first pubescent winter
You seemed very wet and dirty
So I stayed indoors
And acquired a taste
For girls and clean clothes

we found less and less to say
you were jealous so one day
I simply upped and moved away

I still called to see you on occasions
But we had little now in common
And my visits grew less frequent
Until finally
One coldbright April morning
Many years ago
A handful of you
Drummed on my father's
Waxworked coffin

at last it all made sense
there was no need for pretence
you said nothing in defence

And now just recently
While travelling from town to town
Past where you live
I have suddenly become aware
Of you watching me out there
Quietly waiting
Playing patience with the trees

we've avoided eachother for a longtime
and I'm strictly a city man
anytime to call would be the wrong time
I'll avoid you as long as I can.

Tom McGrath

Night Songs

I
to make poems
from bricks
cities
from words

either

a conversation
with a gutter
or a song
to sweep
the streets

i continue
to eat a lot
and sleep
too little

II
yes the madwoman screams
racialism
past my window

the drunk man shouts
that the bastard o'reilly
will tonight
be knifed

yes

the city sickens the heart

gutters do talk

contraceptives and rats

i should have read Mumford
or travelled more

III
the gutters of suburbia
say no more than whispers
behind curtains

the poetry of keyholes

IV
being in the city
i am a junkyard

V
i can continue
because
the night does

regardless

Charles Causley

The Question

In the locked sky beats a dove.
It speaks continually of love.

Deep in the river a talking stone
Says he lies easy who lies alone.

Under the stone there hides a knife:
The beginning and end of every life.

In the dark forest are flowers of light
That never fade by day or night.

Down in the valley stands a tree,
Its roots uneasy as the sea.

High on the tree there hangs a nest.
Here, says the wind, you must take your rest.

Through the spinney with eyes of wax
Runs the woodman with glaring axe.

Naked, my love and I arise
Bathed in his fearful prophecies.

Whose is the bird and whose the stone.
Whose is the light on the midnight sown?

Whose is the tree and whose the rest.
And whose is the knife upon my breast?

Who is the woodman and what does he cry?
Gaze in the mirror. Do not reply.

Anthony Thwaite

Ali Ben Shufti

You want coins? Roman? Greek? Nice vase? Head of god, goddess?
Look, shufti here, very cheap. Two piastres? You joke.

I poke among fallen stones, molehills, the spoil
Left by the archaeologists and carelessly sieved.
I am not above ferreting out a small piece
From the foreman's basket when his back is turned.
One or two of my choicer things were acquired
During what the museum labels call 'the disturbances
Of 1941': you may call it loot,
But I keep no records of who my vendors were—
Goatherds, Johnnies in berets, Neapolitan conscripts
Hot foot out of trouble, dropping a keepsake or two.
I know a good thing, I keep a quiet ear open when
The college bodysnatchers arrive from Chicago,
Florence, Oxford, discussing periods
And measuring everything. I've even done business with them:
You will find my anonymous presence in the excavation reports
When you get to 'Finds Locally Purchased'. Without a B.A.—
And unable to read or write—I can date and price
Any of this rubbish. Here, from my droll pantaloons
That sag in the seat, amusing you no end,
I fetch out Tanagra heads, blue Roman beads,
A Greek lamp, bronze from Byzantium,
A silver stater faced with the head of Zeus.
I know three dozen words of English, enough French
To settle a purchase, and enough Italian
To convince the austere *dottore* he's made a bargain.
As for the past, it means nothing to me but this:
A time when things were made to keep me alive.
You are the ones who go on about it: I survive
By scratching it out with my fingers. I make you laugh
By being obsequious, roguish, battered, in fact
What you like to think of as a typical Arab.
Well, Amr Ibn el-As passed this way
Some thirteen hundred years ago, and we stayed.
I pick over what he didn't smash, and you
Pay for the leavings. That is enough for me.
You take them away and put them on your shelves
And for fifty piastres I give you a past to belong to.

Alan Brownjohn

Farmer's Point of View

I own certain acre-scraps of woodland, scattered
On undulating ground; enough to lie hidden in. So,

About three times a year, and usually August,
Pairs of people come to one or another patch. They stray

Around the edges first, plainly wanting some excuse
To go on in; then talking, as if not concerned,

And always of something else, not what they intend,
They find their way, by one or another approach,

To conducting sexual liaisons—on *my* land.
I've tried to be careful. I haven't mentioned 'love'

Or any idea of passion or consummation;
And I won't call them 'lovers' because I can't say

If they come from affection, or lust, or blackmail,
Or if what they do has any particular point

For either or both (and who can say what 'love' means?)
So what am I saying? I'd like to see people pondering

What unalterable acts they might be committing
When they step down, full of plans, from their trains or cars.

I am not just recording their tragic, or comic, emotions,
Or even the subtler hazards of owning land—

I am honestly concerned. I want to say, politely,
That I worry when I think what they're about:

I want them to explain themselves before they use my woods.

Michael Baldwin

My Position

I read the Crucifixion once a year
And think I understand it. So, of course,
I think they opened God up with a spear
After they'd nailed Him to a wooden cross.

I see a place for Mary, and the Guards,
The woman dabbing with her piece of rag,
Can sympathise with vinegar and cards—
It's my share in the thing that is the snag.

I'm glad He came, as history says, in Nought
And not in nineteen-thirty-one-or-two:
His Presence *now* would put me in a spot,
Just knowing what the hell I'd have to do.

You see, unfortunately, I believe
His message. I'm absolutely sure,
Its great antiquity is my reprieve,
It's been true long enough for me to ignore.

But if He came today and told me Love,
Love Everyone! I know the answer: Kill.
I cannot let this Foreigner remove
The simple satisfactions of my Will.

I'm on the side of Man, and so were they
Who spiked and grunted round His wrists and heels.
Yes—if we had the thing to do today
My smile would bristle with a bunch of nails.

John Moat

Song

My father loved my mother with
Premeditated art
And at his given signal
They tore the earth apart.

But was it his to offer her,
And what was hers to take,
When I was comfortable asleep
Without the will to wake?

My father and my mother were
Cold-blooded man and wife,
They suffered with their one accord
My blind design on life.

Jon Silkin

The Child

Something that can be heard
Is a grasping of soft fingers
Behind that door.
Oh come in, please come in,
And be seated.

It was hard to be sure,
Because for some time a creature
Had bitten at the wood.
But this was something else; a pure noise
Humanly shaped

That gently insists on
Being present. I am sure you are.
Look: the pots over the fire
On a shelf, just put;
So, and no other way,

Are as you have seen them; and you,
Being visible, make them no different.
No man nor thing shall take
Your place from you; so little,
You would think, to ask for.

I have not denied; you know that.
Do you? Do you see
How you are guttered
At a breath, a flicker from me?
Burn more then.

Move this way with me,
Over the stone. Here are
Your father's utensils on
The kitchen wall; cling
As I lead you.

It seems you have come without speech
And flesh. If it be love
That moves with smallness through
These rooms, speak to me,
As you move.

You have not come with
Me, but burn on the stone.

If I could pick you up
If I could lift you;
Can a thing be weightless?
I have seen, when I did lift you

How your flesh was casually
Pressed in. You have come
Without bone, or blood.
Is that to be preferred?
A flesh without

Sinew, a bone that has
No hardness, and will not snap.
Hair with no spring; without
Juices, touching, or speech.
What are you?

Or rather, show me, since
You cannot speak, that you are real;
A proper effusion of air,
Not that I doubt, blown by a breath
Into my child;

As if you might grow on that vapour
To thought, or natural movement
That expresses, 'I know where I am.'
Yet that you are here,
I feel.

Though you are different.
The brain being touched lightly,
It was gone. Yet since you live,
As if you were not born,
Strangeness of strangeness, speak.

Or rather, touch my breath
With your breath, steadily
And breathe yourself into me.

The soft huge pulsing comes
And passes through my flesh
Out of my hearing.

Jon Stallworthy

The Almond Tree

I

All the way to the hospital
the lights were green as peppermints.
Trees of black iron broke into leaf
ahead of me, as if
I were the lucky prince
in an enchanted wood
summoning summer with my whistle,
banishing winter with a nod.

Swung by the road from bend to bend,
I was aware that blood was running
down through the delta of my wrist
and under arches
of bright bone. Centuries,
continents it had crossed;
from an undisclosed beginning
spiralling to an unmapped end.

II

Crossing (at sixty) Magdalen Bridge
Let it be son, a son, said
the man in the driving mirror,
Let it be a son. The tower
held up its hand: the college
bells shook their blessing on his head.

III

I parked in an almond's
shadow blossom, for the tree
was waving, waving me
upstairs with a child's hands.

IV

Up
the spinal stair
and at the top
along
a bone-white corridor
the blood tide swung
me swung me to a room
whose walls shuddered
with the shuddering womb.

Under the sheet
wave after wave, wave
after wave beat
on the bone coast, bringing
ashore—whom?
               New-
minted, my bright farthing!
Coined by our love, stamped with
our images, how you
enrich us! Both
you make one. Welcome
to your white sheet,
my best poem!

V

At seven-thirty
the visitors' bell
scissored the calm
of the corridors.
The doctor walked with me
to the slicing doors.

His hand upon my arm,
his voice—*I have to tell
you*—set another bell
beating in my head:
your son is a mongol
the doctor said.

VI

How easily the word went in—
clean as a bullet
leaving no mark on the skin,
stopping the heart within it.

This was my first death.
The '*I*' ascending on a slow
last thermal breath
studied the man below

as a pilot treading air might
the buckled shell of his plane—
boot, glove, and helmet
feeling no pain

from the snapped wires' radiant ends.
Looking down from a thousand feet
I held four walls in the lens
of an eye; wall, window, the street

a torrent of windscreens, my own
car under its almond tree,
and the almond waving me down.
I wrestled against gravity,
but light was melting and the gulf
cracked open. Unfamiliar
the body of my late self
I carried to the car.

VII

The hospital—its heavy freight
lashed down ship-shape ward over ward—
steamed into night with some on board
soon to be lost if the desperate

charts were known. Others would come
altered to land or find the land
altered. At their voyage's end
some would be added to, some

diminished. In a numbered cot
my son sailed from me; never to come
ashore into my kingdom
speaking my language. Better not

look that way. The almond tree
was beautiful in labour. Blood-
dark, quickening, bud after bud
split, flower after flower shook free.

On the darkening wind a pale
face floated. Out of reach. Only when
the buds, all the buds, were broken
would the tree be in full sail.

In labour the tree was becoming
itself. I, too, rooted in earth
and ringed by darkness, from the death
of myself saw myself blossoming,

wrenched from the caul of my thirty
years' growing, fathered by my son,
unkindly in a kind season
by love shattered and set free

VIII

You turn to the window for the first time.
I am called to the cot
To see your focus shift,
take tendril-hold on a shaft
of sun, explore its dusty surface, climb
to an eye you cannot

meet. You have a sickness they cannot heal,
the doctors say: locked in
your body you will remain.
Well, I have been locked in mine.
We will tunnel each other out. You seal
the covenant with a grin.

In the days we have known one another,
my little mongol love,
I have learnt more from your lips
than you will from mine perhaps:
I have learnt that to live is to suffer,
to suffer is to live.

Jon Stallworthy

Letters to my Sisters

Asleep till nine, again you break
Your croissants by the tideless lake
Where small fish quarrel for crumbs
And, making with its paddle-beat
No more stir than a swan's feet,
The day's first steamer comes

Obliquely to the landing stage.
At ten you walk into the village
For the long hot loaves and cheese
To be eaten as you lie
Halfway to a Renaissance sky
Among the crocuses and bees.

As my days have been, your day is.
Cowbells and churchbell and the kiss
Of scythes in tilting pastures shake
The web of silence, but your look
Travels seldom from your book.
The sun takes a turn round the lake.

Only when evening throws the last
Steamer like a dart burning past
The point, and ghostly waiters
Whisper that supper is soon,
Will you stumble down as the moon
Stumbles on the tideless waters.

The moon is a periscope in which
An exile like myself may watch,
Over mountains rough as broken glass,
Others who prepare to make
Their longest journey from the lake
Into the formidable pass.

All see only the green incline.
So many have crossed that skyline
Singing, and none of them come back
To tell how night in the ravine
Cut them off like a guillotine,
Still there is singing on the track.

Darkness and mist and the false echo
Divide the singers, and snow
Cancels each step. Some as they clamber
Lonely over glaciers find,
Imprisoned under ice, a friend
Like an insect in green amber.

But here the sun, in rising, makes
Bonfires of the embattled peaks.
Winds have sung with us: and we
In exultation have seen,
Distant but luminous between
Mountain and mountain, the tidal sea.

Little sisters, about to climb
Beyond your valley for the first time,
What can I give you—talisman
Or map—that may guide you straight
Into a plain as temperate
As the valley where we began?

Not my example, certainly.
Only my love—and this: I see,
Whenever the going is rough,
Those who defy foul weather
And avalanche are roped together
And the rope is love.

Alan Bold

A Memory of Death

Nineteen fifty six was a momentous year,
The year of Suez and Hungary and the death
Of my father. I was thirteen. He was forty-nine.
His body stiffened in the quarry for a day or so,
His flesh submerged and became bloated
While I sat at home full of premonitions of his death.
It seemed the most natural thing for him to die,
The fitting conclusion to the warnings
And daily visits from genial policemen.
Four days we waited, then the news. Dead.
Found dead in the quarry. Circumstances unknown.
Cause of death: asphyxia due to drowning.

'William Bold/Clerk of Works/ (Dept. of Agric. for Scot.)/ . . . 1956/
March/ Found drowned in Bigbreck Quarry,/Twatt, Birsay, about
4.30 p.m. on Sunday 18th/March 1956. Last seen alive about 6.30 p.m.
on/Wednesday 14th March 1956. . . .'

I remember how the letters to my mother brought back
That summer on the farm in Orkney. The cabin.
The cottage. Living between the cabin and the cottage.
It was the one time I had him to myself.
On the farm Hazel used to take me in her bed at night.
I clung to her big body and felt her warm
Limbs. Hazel was kind and rather slow
And she never said much. But each night
She let me share her bed to get warmth.
She could dribble warm milk down my mouth,
Drive a tractor and decapitate
A hen. Only she could milk the cows expertly,
Gripping their udders with her weather-beaten hands
Laughing as if she had everything anyone could want.
Her presence gave me comfort like a field of corn.
Her voice familiar as the motors threshing,
As the dogs running and barking. Once,
I fell in the cowshed. I stank
With the sloppy excrement plastered all over.
But she threw her big-boned torso round me,
Washed me down and grasped me and smiled
And the sun shone through her mane of hair.
On the same cow she sat me and held me tight.

And at night we would gape at the moon
Silently fixing our thoughts on it, Hazel
With her arms round me, smiling, glowing,
And we would go to bed after porridge and cocoa.

'I can't tell you how sorry I am to hear of your sad loss . . . I pray that
God be with you to give you strength to bear your great loss.'

Snick-crack! The shot was fired. Whirr
Of wings and beat of leaves and shadows in the night.
My first time pulling the trigger. The lake.
Undulating blackness catching shreds of light.
I giggled with the sensation of accomplishment.
He winked and grinned. Then into the boat.
Silently we sliced through the black water.
We didn't speak but listened to the ripples.
Then the illegal otter was launched: a length
Of rope decorated with murderous hooks and, sleek
As an otter, the streamlined wood that pulled the rope.
We waited, looking at each other, grinning
Conspiratorially. Then the jerk and pull
And rip! The mouth snaps and the lip pouts
And we've got a trout. A gleaming trout, a trout
Of subtle highlights and I thump its lovely head
Hard against an oar. One down and several
To go. It's up to us. No rush. Our choice.
Guilty—and happy. Cold—but flushed. Two—like one.

At the farm we grilled the trout. They sizzled away
And we slobbered after them. He thumbed to me.
'He'll make a good poacher, this one, some day!'
Cosy and loveable farm, in an hour or so the sun
Will show. The lake will sparkle and we can look
But no one else will know.

'How is Alan? I suppose he will soon be giving work a thought as well.
What a shame to think he doesn't have his Dad to start him off and such
a clever man.'

Fiddle music, stomping feet, thrills
Whisky flowing, boozed up to the gills,
Children on the floor and cakes,
Party pieces, old repeated jokes.

Laughter linking kids and wives and daft
Workers clumping joyously on soft
Carpets—kisses innocent as sweets,
Embraces making boys and girls mates.

Secrets shared and little stories told
Peat thrown on the fire against the cold.
An old piano, floorboards worn and dark
And folk united through the heavy work.

It finishes too soon, the morning calls
And blankets cover all internal ills.
A passer-by will see another farm
Oblivious to the life that breaks the storm.

And inside as the shutters shake and creak
A child's eyes eagerly wait for day to break
And look hard for another night like this
Hoping to God the present doesn't pass.

'I never for one minute thought Bill would come to such an end. I
always admired his carefree personality . . . God knows best and that's
all we can say about it.'

A lot has been written about Skara Brae,
Vivid first-hand impressions made on the spot.
Full of mystery or a stern sense of history,
Or perhaps some blots scrawled on the back of a postcard
In the pub.
I have a feeling for the place now, rather than a picture.
We had been building a bridge,
Watching the digger devastating the earth,
Waving off the midgies and the clegs.
And after the morning's work: Skara Brae.
I saw burials older than I will ever be.
Remarkable reconstructions of the primitive way of life.
Immaculate patterns of rooms from stone.
The evidence of ingenuity, the suggestion
Of a rigid way of life. And the whole thing
Deep in the ground.
It did not seem amazing or beautiful.
It seemed preposterous in comparison with the farm.
And, perhaps worst of all, it was invaded by new people,
Empty of the old inhabitants. I remember thinking that.
I often think of it now as a silent tomb
For those we never could have known and never try
To know. He was there and it sticks now.
It is redolent with memorial melodies,
A monument made from destruction.
And when I saw Skara Brae
In that clear afternoon, my muscles aching,
I saw it as a member of posterity.

'. . . although he was only a lodger his tragic death has upset me terrible. As you know he was his own worst friend he certainly was indulging in spirits too much . . . all we can do is bless him from the bottom of our hearts and remember his happy smile.'

I remember his happy smile.
I remember the gaps of missing teeth, the black
Spots on the white, the large lower lip,
I remember the fairisle pullover, green and rust
And white, the ruddy face, the twisted arm broken
In a car crash. I remember the way he walked
Like a big ape
His jacket open, flapping, his eyes bright.

I remember too the alcoholic breath, the false
Euphoria and, after rumbling into chasms of distress,
Depression and confessions of guilt.
These no longer matter, though they seemed to matter then.
They mattered more than they should have. It is so
In Scotland, land of the omnipotent No.

The Sunday-school picnic, the twittering old birds,
The benevolent boy-scouts, the ministers dripping
With goodwill. And the disgrace. He was drunk.
Not objectionable. Just dead drunk.
Sprawled out on the grass focusing on the sky,
With whispers hissing maliciously round about.
They were well pleased with something to feel superior
About, with half a chance to gloat.
'Do you mind Mr. Bold?' What! Grunt!
'Do you mind Mr. Bold not lying there?' Mmmm!
'Do you think you could stand up?'
He tried to, tried so hard, so ostentatiously,
Arms working like a tightrope walker's,
Legs unbuckling—then thump.
Down and out.

'. . . it was a huge shock to us all after being here so long with us he was in here so short before having a talk with Jim my husband and the rest of them it was a cold day and I made tea to them all sitting round the fire I think he missed the cabin as they all used to call it he could take a rest when he wanted . . .'

He left the land rover
And stared deep into the water
Thinking life offered nothing more than this liquid pit.
Everything shrunk to the need for action,
For decision. And the audacity of the stars.

Everything at such a distance, people, family,
Friends. And headlong he fell
Slowly into the water
And swore in bubbles
And his eyelids filled with blackness.

Robert Nye

Fishing

At thirteen he went fishing for stars.
Either for lack of hooks or love of the strict twine
Which could be taught to shiver in the hand
He fished for them, saying he fished for crabs.

No bait gets glory. He used mussels.
After school he had searched the hard
And taken plenty when the tide was out;
Now each agape, its matter manifest,
His greed made fast with a half-Gordian knot
In a new context, and sent back to the dark
About its tacit business. He felt sure
Some star that lurked or smouldered in the net
Of stars below the surface could be caught.

Crab after crab came up, acknowledging
His wasteful magic and his innocence,
But still no star rose clinging to a shell.
Once, twice, he thought he had one, but
Only an unlucky starfish floundered, half-wound
In the sea-stained twine, mocking star-need.
Sick of ambition, cold with self-deceit,
He lost his sleight of hand, let all his gear
Ride with the tide, and sat and watched the moon.

Later he learned how not to fish too much—
Or, rather, how to fish for more than stars
With less than mussels or a singing line.
He fished for nothing. And he caught the sea.

Michael Baldwin

Recognition

If I parted a hair, found a clock
And there was the bone ticking in it,
If I dug up the sun from a pool
And discovered the heart of time:

Would I know this bone and this heart,
Would I know they were hers?
Does it matter? I dig no pool,
I part no hairs.

John Moat

Three Trees

Somewhere I read the aloe tree—
White bloom above, deep shade beneath,
With bitter sap and spiky leaf—
Will only flower one year in three.
Love flowers like the aloe tree.

Her wattle cut for wizardry,
There in the coven of the wood
The gods feed on her poison blood,
Her berries red for all to see—
Love's fruit hangs on the rowan tree.

Somebody once described for me
The lenten purple of the shoot,
The tarnished gold flung at the root,
A gallows white for treachery!
Love flowers like the judas tree.

Brian Patten

Diary Poem

We sit here, twenty; drunk. Wind and stars
gush in through the skylight. We sense
in the air how winter's coming
and how our lives and those that surround them
have frozen. We sit, neither sane nor mad,
outside in a room we'll never enter
our first crime, a child, bawls out,
shakes a fist in anger. Inside us
sad and lonely creatures wander,
looking for an exit from themselves. They
are more important now than the shapes we wear.
Those shapes are not unique.

We have sent out frantic messages, covering
the city, all its men, its women.
Yet those few who came forward did not move us.
Confined by faith to a flower that's perishing
we move, frozen not by these seasons
but by our own weather. It's inside us
that the years pour.

Then perhaps it is best that we wake expecting little,
feel no more need to exaggerate ourselves
nor perform those rituals that have ceased to amaze us,
but washed by the morning's first light
to drift out into the city, one thought
in its still sleeping brain. . . . And yet
on waking we find
that longing for something other than our own shapes
grows continually, eats away at all other things till
one seemingly unperishable thing is left—
it is the need of each other, is love
the bruised shape we pick
from now freezing orchards.

Anthony Thwaite

Personal Effects

Unable to travel light, I carry
Unnecessary luggage here and there.
To live out of a suitcase, to be free
Of everything but a toothbrush and the fare—
Admirable, but I can't imagine how
Such people can ever have an anywhere
They call their own, and without that I know
Life would be a burden I couldn't bear.

So here, among the pyjamas and the socks,
I stow away a talisman or two,
And label that huge metal-lined travelling-box
Personal Effects, which may not seem true
Enough to convince the Customs, but is so.
An affluent magpie in a nest that creaks
With impedimenta, everywhere I go
I lug an accumulation of years or weeks.

Odd that a man with so much need of roots
Restlessly plucks them up, weighing a ton,
And finds that burdened travel somehow suits
His nature and his situation.
Naked we enter the world and naked we leave it,
So I have heard, and take it as true enough;
Yet no matter how reason and faith believe it,
Off I go, loaded with perishable stuff.

D. M. *Black*

With Decorum

I lay down and having
died, gave my instructions: they
filled the room with
balloons and streamers, cherubim at the four
corners of the ceiling blowing their bright bugles—
laid me on a carved catafalque, in an
embroidered robe
crusted with emeralds; doctor and
priest in black mantles;
inconsolable women. Trundling of
wheels, the entire
building moves to the cemetery. Seagulls are
crying at the shut window. The ba-
lloons joggle.
           I sit up and bellow: Death,
then it is
time for the
party!—we
draw decanters out of the coffin, tear in our
teeth the candy lilies; ah the
trumpets' Reveille, the
rollicking floor! Open the
windows, Jock! My
beauties, my
noble horses—yoked in
pairs, white horses, drawing my great
hearse, galloping and
frolicking over the cropped turf.

Geoffrey Hill

Annunciations

1

The Word has been abroad, is back, with a tanned look
From its subsistence in the stiffening-mire.
Cleansing has become killing, the reward
Touchable, overt, clean to the touch.
Now at a distance from the steam of beasts,
The loathly neckings and fat shook spawn
(Each specimen-jar fed with delicate spawn)
The searchers with the curers sit at meat
And are satisfied. Such precious things put down
And the flesh eased through turbulence the soul
Purples itself; each eye squats full and mild
While all who attend to fiddle or to harp
For betterment, flavour their decent mouths
With gobbets of the sweetest sacrifice.

2

O Love, subject of the mere diurnal grind,
Forever being pledged to be redeemed,
Expose yourself for charity; be assured
The body is but husk and excrement.
Enter these deaths according to the law,
O visited women, possessed sons! Foreign lusts
Infringe our restraints; the changeable
Soldiery have their goings-out and comings-in
Dying in abundance. Choicest beasts
Suffuse the gutters with their colourful blood.
Our God scatters corruption. Priests, martyrs,
Parade to this imperious theme: 'O Love,
You know what pains succeed; be vigilant; strive
To recognize the damned among your friends.'

Peter Levi sj

Pancakes for the Queen of Babylon

I

Branches of green in trees of darker green

they ran barefoot
they have thrown away their shoes.

Footprint of a star.

I was hungry all night;
I was thirsty all night.
One of them will bring water in her hand,
another will bring berries in his hand

the desert
stirring again
the dust of revolutionary wars.

Sleeping sometimes in the foliage of the vineyard

The darkness hand in hand with the darkness.
I am a secret mountain
tenebrous, flea-bitten by starlight,
my eyes are gone:
then when you cut my throat it bleeds coffee
with a trickle of alcohol.

I am unable to wake
in the vine's thin foliage only fumble
for the dregs of night at the breast of the darkness.

And one hoof of a star printing the dark
is ringing like a nail of a new metal.

II

Midnight wrings out its withering sunset
I clutch my violet, it smells of garlic
and sleep heavy.
Confusion is bluer than violets.

The law is already an antique:
it is always older than when you woke,
you are unable to say how you know it;
the law is older
                is a given thing
                          and when I wake
waking will be as deep as the dream was

Waking is walking,
is to wake to find
a cold violet coast in a green waste,
where a black horse in bud and a white horse
are chewing down the piebald rose-bushes.

My law is this confusion:
if it were not obscure how could I wake?
The law is an old question
which was over before we were awake.

We woke to find
a white boat rocking on black water
a black wind rocking on white water
a white boat rocking on black water

III

To speak about the soul.
I wake early. You don't sleep in summer.
In the morning a dead-eyed nightingale is still awake in you.
What has been done and suffered
with whatever is left to be suffered
is in the soul.
Oracles are given elsewhere. Their speech is associated with bronze.

In the early morning
you see women walking to the sanctuaries:
a light touch of sun on the whitewash:
a light touch of fire burning the oil.
You tell me nothing.
This is the desert I will write about.
The desert is not an island: the island is not enchanted: and the
                              desert is no habitation for men.
The bird with the burnt eyes sang sweetest.
a desert further off
One small simple cloud. Heat at midday. A little constellated hand-
                            writing. Heat at midnight.

You never say.
To be woken by hearing
the voices of the enchanted birds
and the voices of disenchanted birds.

Say what is like a tree, like a river, like a mountain, a cloud over
the sun?

My memory has been overshadowed
by that live light and by that dying light.

The soul is no more than human.

The rising sky is as wide as the desert.

George Mackay Brown

The Finished House

In the finished house, a flame is brought to the hearth.
Then a table, between door and window
Where a stranger will eat before the men of the house.
A bed is laid in a secret corner
For the three agonies—love, birth, death—
That are made beautiful with ceremony.
The neighbours come with gifts—
A set of cups, a calendar, some chairs,
A fiddle is hung at the wall.
A girl puts lucky salt in a dish.
The cupboard has its loaf and bottle.
On the seventh morning
One spills water of blessing over the threshold.

Ted Hughes

Second Glance at a Jaguar

Skinfull of bowls, he bowls them,
The hip going in and out of joint, dropping the spine
With the urgency of his hurry
Like a cat going along under thrown stones, under cover,
Glancing sideways, running
Under his spine. A terrible, stump-legged waddle
Like a thick Aztec disemboweller,
Club-swinging, trying to grind some square
Socket between his hind legs round,
Carrying his head like a brazier of spilling embers,
And the black bit of his mouth, he takes it
Between his back teeth, he has to wear his skin out,
He swipes a lap at the water-trough as he turns,
Swivelling the ball of his heel on the polished spot,
Showing his belly like a butterfly,
At every stride he has to turn a corner
In himself and correct it. His head
Is like the worn down stump of another whole jaguar,
His body is just the engine shoving it forward,
Lifting the air up and shoving on under,
The weight of his fangs hanging the mouth open,
Bottom jaw combing the ground. A gorged look,
Gangster, club-tail lumped along behind gracelessly,
He's wearing himself to heavy ovals,
Muttering some mantrah, some drum-song of murder
To keep his rage brightening, making his skin
Intolerable, spurred by the rosettes, the cain-brands,
Wearing the spots off from the inside,
Rounding some revenge. Going like a prayer-wheel,
The head dragging forward, the body keeping up,
The hind legs lagging. He coils, he flourishes
The blackjack tail as if looking for a target,
Hurrying through the underworld, soundless.

Christopher Logue

Cats are full of Death

Cats are full of death.
Horses
and even very small dogs
scare me.
I fear I am not very English.
Lately, however,
a mouse has come to live in my flat.
At forty, pushing forty-one,
a man who lives alone
and breaks his teeth whilst eating jam
is, is he not,
rather ridiculous?
So I am grateful.
I eat at home more often,
compose with greater ease,
and yesterday I bought a book on mice.

Really, he's very fortunate;
though poor I have expensive tastes,
my mouse has camembert and brie in peace
whereas some mice of my acquaintance run
fantastic risks
for cubes of greasy cheddar.

I must admit he's not all that intelligent;
the first time I saw him
walking down the middle of the room
tail in the air
Tra-La!
I thought he was brave.
Now I realize he had lost his hole.
Later I discovered he had only one eye,
and, needless to say,
posh vets won't have him in their surgeries.
What's more
Madame won't like him.
But what can you do?
He has moved in
and she hasn't.

Neither Nor

I would neither love nor hate
But sad for me I learned too late
That I must either love or hate.

I would neither live nor die.
I want to watch a distant sky.
Yet I live and I will die.

I would be neither young nor old
Though the sun is mine and gold
I am young who will be old.

I would be neither poor nor rich
The football pool's a fecund ditch
The penny's poor that makes me rich.

I would neither sink nor swim
And yet the water has this whim
That I must either sink or swim.

O half by half and two by two
I am bisected through and through
By all the things I couldn't do.

D. M. Thomas

The Lost Forest

I look at a garden turned to tussock and bramble,
hazed in a sudden carn-mist.
My love wore yellow yesterday,
love wore yellow.

Where my father warns my ball-chasing
legs from new-raked earth,
my daughter stands, giggling, lost,
as in a jungle.

Could he but see her, he'd toss her high!
but no more to him than this sea-wood
I gather for a study paperweight.
The pain of loss conceived her, branch for root.

She giggles . . . 'I had a bad dream, daddy.
Do you want to hear it?
Your arms and legs were broken off and
Gran got smaller and smaller!'

Where St Petroc prayed and Wesley preached,
we drink cocktails, surf laps the sunlounge.
My love wore yellow yesterday,
love wore yellow.

Glad to get away for an evening
from the woman cobwebbed with pain, fat with
crippled inaction, whose empire's shrunk
each time I come, each summer.

Her pain's loving, unchallengeable
tedium I can't bear to watch,
it's boring us, all that stealthy decline.
My love wore yellow.

Maybe when what empire is left
of her once dominant atlas-flag
(a chair, a radio now) has dis-coloured
to nothing, grows all commonwealth,

and I am sent for, some night, a sleeker car
called to move into third-gear to
descend this tin-coombe of grey crumbling
stacks, and flooded shafts, the one unfailing pilot-light

calling across the sea-rainy deep,
posthumously and for the last time,
come home to stand formally as
chaos uproots me from my self, my inheritance,

and to set a match to the certificates
in the tin-box hidden to all but me,
(yesterday my love wore white,
my love wore white)

I'll be able to face her again, gladly,
see, in the double-photo I unhook from the wall,
the woman my father came back to
from the States—the taste of her

faithful, saffron-moist, tangy kiss!—
already she's younger than me! Desirable!
Or younger-looking still, beyond desire,
a child clutching her Monday copper-guinea,

she and five brothers, racing to the corner-shop . . .

We stop on a hill, the town below dense.
Out from Mount's Bay
the lost forest, lost jungle strides.

Roger McGough

The Fight of the Year

'And there goes the bell for the third month
and Winter comes out of its corner looking groggy
Spring leads with a left to the head
followed by a sharp right to the body
    daffodils
    primroses
    crocuses
    snowdrops
    lilacs
    violets
    pussywillow
Winter can't take much more punishment
and Spring shows no signs of tiring
    tadpoles
    squirrels
    baalambs
    badgers
    bunny rabbits
    mad march hares
    horses and hounds
Spring is merciless
Winter won't go the full twelve rounds
    bobtail clouds
    scallywaggy winds
    the sun
    a pavement artist
    in every town
A left to the chin
and Winter's down!
 1   tomatoes
 2   radish
 3   cucumber
 4   onions
 5   beetroot
 6   celery
 7   and any
 8   amount
 9   of lettuce
10   for dinner
Winter's out for the count
Spring is the winner!'

Edward Lucie-Smith

The May-Fly

This little fly
Lives just a day
And dances all
His hours away.

Better, like him,
To die tomorrow
Than live for cent-
Uries in sorrow.

George Mackay Brown

Horse

The horse at the shore
Casks of red apples, skull, a barrel of rum

The horse in the field
Plough, ploughman, gulls, a furrow, a cornstalk

The horse in the peat-bog
Twelve baskets of dark fire

The horse at the pier
Letters, bread, paraffin, one passenger, papers

The horse at the show
Ribbons, raffia, high bright hooves

The horse in the meadow
A stallion, a red wind, between the hills

The horse at the burn
Quenching a long flame in the throat

Lemmings

Lemmings die every year. Over the cliff
They pour, hot blood into cold sea,
So that you half imagine steam
Will rise. They do not part company
At first, but spread out, a brown team
Like seaweed, undulant and tough.

Light changes, and the wind may veer
As they swim out and on. The sea
May become sleek or shrewish. Foam
May blind them or may let them see
The wet horizon. It takes time.
They do not die within an hour.

One by one they leave the air
And drown as individuals.
From minute to minute they blink out
Like aeroplanes or stars or gulls
Whose vanishing is never caught.
All in time will disappear.

And though their vitality
Does not look morbid enough
People call it suicide
Which it has some appearance of.
But it may well be that the mood
In which each year these lemmings die

Is nothing worse than restlessness,
The need to change and nothing else.
They have learnt this piece of strand
So thoroughly it now seems false.
They jump, thinking there is land
Beyond them, as indeed there is.

Paul Roche

Mother Goose gone Grim

Megadeath and Overkill
Went down to the sea with laughter
Megadeath dried up the clouds
And Overkill the water.

Megadeath and Overkill
Went to the skies to slaughter
Megadeath came tumbling down
And Overkill soon after.

Robert Nye

A Bat in a Box

The long cold cracked and I walked in the cracks
To pay the rent for the first time in weeks
And pick our post up from the farm on the top road

That done—'Has your son,' said the farmer's wife
'Ever seen a bat in a box? I have one
You could take back to show him.'

And I imagined how a bat in a box
Would beat its bloodshot wings, and comb itself
With greedy claws, and eat up flies and beetles;

And how, when hanging by the wing-hooks, it
Would sleep, long ears tucked under, as if cloaked:
And how its tameness might in fact confound me.

I did not take it, back down through snow
To the lukewarm hearth.
                              Why did I not do so?

To tell you, I would have to undo winter,
Thaw my bare heart, waste its bitterness,
Losing the wry frost with some deeper drifts.

A bat,
        in a box.
                    Just think of it.

Jack Clemo

Gulls Nesting Inland

You herring-gulls on truant flight
From sea that roars like dynamite
Find soft blue water, cliffs peeled white.

A cosy world that apes the real,
Where clanging tides can never steal,
Nor salty fangs of spume congeal.

This breeding-ground yields more repose
Than wave-scoured rocks from Looe to Zoze;
But mildness cheats where nothing flows.

I watch you dip your beaks and wings
In water risen from pit-bed springs
That hold no finny shimmerings.

Though you may change your habits here,
You will not see the shoals appear:
No herring feast in claywork sphere.

You are like us who try to school
Our spirits in some sheltered pool,
Fathomed and tideless, never cruel,

Where knowledge bounded and secure
Refreshed us till we shed the lure
Of maddening currents, depths obscure.

But though we choose clay mimicry
Our proper food lies in a sea
Of perilous infinity.

John Moat

Four Quarters

The wind has moved South
I don't recall when
I slept one moment
The garden turned green
The blackbird last evening
Sang it was spring
But this morning the cuckoo
And she has gone.

The wind has moved East
The year's growing old
I caught her whisper
The garden turned gold
The cuckoo last evening
Called summer in
But this morning the robin
And she has gone.

The wind has moved North
Its teeth are laid bare
I searched the garden
Found nobody there
The robin last evening
Cheaped autumn's song
But this morning the raven
And she has gone.

The wind has moved West
It shifted last night
I woke this morning
The garden was white
The raven last evening
Croaked winter home
But this morning the blackbird
And she has gone.

Michael Mackmin

Alter and Invent

I thought I'd send you flowers,
I thought yellow
daffodils,

you cannot
think to
go.

you
have an
ideal, a
carved
heart, held
crystal, no
I will not
imagine
tell me, tell
me,

you cannot
think to
go.

even the sky
has planes, the flats & angles,
cones, obelisks,
gigantic
shafts
where colour strikes colour,

even the sky
& even life.

you cannot
think to
go.

the shape of breath
is kissing,

burst your heart,
bowl and pummel
the woollen
clouds of nightmare
in your mind,

do not
think to go,

shift
as the coloured sky
dances as a lark
dances,

ease &
slide in, kiss,
the shape of breath
is kissing.

and I
in the stone & rock,
& floating sky,
have
an ideal,
the structure

that we make
with love
that falls, & that
we make again, softly,
for an ideal
is a bending
heart.

I thought I'd send you
flowers
I thought yellow
daffodils.

Roger McGough

Poem about the sun slinking off and pinning up a notice

the sun
hasn't got me fooled
not for a minute
just when
you're beginning to believe
that   grass is green
and   skies are blue
and   colour is king
hey   ding a ding ding
and

      a

          host

               of

                    other

                        golden

                              etceteras

before you know where you are
he's slunk off somewhere
and pinned up a notice saying:

    MOON

John Fairfax

Moonsong

Rise through the sky
To the moon way above
I spin on my couch
From the earth that I love.

O I will walk
On the grey tranquil sea
Casting no shadow
Seeking no mystery.

I'll gather dust
And some diamond rock
To give blue Earth
For her jealous stock.

Don't look for me
Singing over your head
Join the moonsong
And our freefalling tread.

Orpheus is here
In gold-tinted dome,
Icarus left
On his long way home.

We have marked the track
Through orbital bar
And sung our way
To this lonely star.

Now raise your eyes
And your voice and your hands
The moon has danced
To Apollo's band.

O rise through space
To the stars way above
Spin on your couches
From the blue Earth you love.

D. M. Black

Document of an Inter-Stellar Journey

The imagination contracts. The cold is outside. Roy, in
18 years, will
barely grow older.

enclosed pellet . . .

He goes to and fro, winding yarn off the hoops of the dashboard. He
is knitting blankets. Time
killed is deployed as usefully as by my
lurching thought

We have put the constellations awry. A screen
re-creates the sky to us. Taurus approaches; the Plough wrenches apart

neither up nor down. The stable
whirl in circles. The unstable
arc by the porthole at
any angle—our own
course at odds with the lot o them

a chosen path;
ex-chosen;
among this machinery

The retardation of watches we can
make allowance for. I
carve earth's weeks on the rim of the table. A day
takes almost no-time—
                                    well, say
8 hours

The psychologists were of course in error: it's
hesitant journeys only that
lead to neurosis. Happy as dogs we
watch the progress chart.

What cubic volume, that was before, we put behind us!

Roy is going mad. He stands at the screen, tapping the
main stars with the tips of his fingers. As he
does so, making a
soft, exploding noise. *Pow!* We got him! Out, you
bastard, out! *Pow!* And so on.

67

the food wd drive anyone scatty. A range of labels, all
meaning oxtail or carrots. Or cocoa. For a
pint of heavy and peanuts I would

this bloody carpet

The door would hardly shut, the key would
hardly turn. I am glad to
take over Roy's place, my
feet on the chest of dials. O, we advance!

enclosed nut, falling thro' space.
                              It is
my posture also. I revive acquaintance with the nature of solitude. He,
                                                                    tho'
scrabbling at the door from time to time, is
not violent

From the lee of the steel
shield the blast is shifted beyond me. My warmth dives thro' its cold.
                                                                  My air
is calm, rich; but it
sparse and a tempest. Did I not
lack courage—

But whatever
comes I shall have
had this arena. Terribly small
compatible band, between the blast and the wreckage. I
arrange the ornaments, eaten with gloom.

The Plough is out of shape; and Cassiopeia
unrecognisable

vast wilderness. Even the blast
a
thread, in that stagnant ocean

Mistake, that is my thought. A slip-up of atoms
led to this quavering flesh, without place
in the reckless tempest of matter. Unnatural
being, these straggling molecules, this
lust for togetherness—I
mean on their part

I prepare two gallons of soup. It will keep him going. He has
anyway abandoned feeding.

what
beauty: the slow welling out of the depths of the oxtail! the
odor

That life is bad, and not to be
rendered otherwise there have been
staunch men to accept. I
can neither
accept nor think it. By
action, trial, frenzy
we can undo—

I sit in front of the soup. I grow light-headed. Roy, by
way of the key-holes looks
catatonic

my purpose, Jesus!

An inner
door will have to be sealed. The lining
strips from its rim. I
clear to the hatches

I go back in. I unlock his door. He
crouches haggard under the wash-basin, against the
pipe
tho' I
drag the soup to his doorway. Soup, Roy, soup. There is
no reaction.

He will emerge, when the
time is ripe. I come, my splendour. Upright, swiftly, I
go to the door

Sealing it back the
full chill begins to impinge. Only the hatches
now keep me from my world. I
break their vacuous tension